Hilda's Story

Surviving the Holocaust

Edited by Lori Krein
Granddaughter of Hilda

Copyright 2024 by Lori Krein
Version #: 10/29/2024

Published by Mariposa Publishing

ISBN: 978-1-7374599-6-5
(paperback)

Memoir of Hilda Thieberger
Written and edited by Lori Krein

Forward

This book is based on a series of interviews with my grandmother, Hilda Thieberger, for the Oral History Project, Jewish Community Council of Greater Washington on July 25, 1989.

The Holocaust was the systematic, state-sponsored persecution and murder of six million Jews by the Nazi regime and its allies and collaborators. The US Holocaust Memorial Museum teaches millions of people each year about the dangers of unchecked hatred and the need to prevent genocide.

I decided to transcribe my Grandmother's stories because although it's more intimate hearing/watching her tell the stories first hand, in her own voice, via YouTube or the audio recordings from the Jewish Community Council of Greater Washington, it's sometimes difficult to follow along.

I took on this project as a labor of love, and as a gift to my family. I believe it's important that we have, in writing, a record of these events. My grandparents and my mother came close to death many times during the war, but through sheer determination, resourcefulness, and the help of others, they survived.

Disclaimer: Although I did my best to verify the dates and places Hilda shared, there are some discrepancies, missing links, and contradictory information.

"The purpose of creating this living memorial is to add to the oral history of the Nazi Holocaust so that future generations will know what happened. With this knowledge, hopefully, we can prevent any such occurrence in the future." - United States Holocaust Museum

Table of Contents

Introduction/summary

Hidegard (Hilda) Goldberger was born in February of 1913 in Teschen, a border town near southern Poland. [*Polish: Cieszyn, Czech: Těšina)* The town was half Czech and half Polish, and she had a Czech passport. Teschen, an eastern European city, was divided by Poland and Czechoslovakia after World War I. Hilda was born on the Czech side; on the east bank of the Olza River. Hilda married **Erwin Thieberger** in November, 1935, and gave birth to their daughter **Renee** in February, 1937 in Bilitz, Poland. She bore two more children; **Hanna**, in 1945; and **Julie**, in 1956.

Through their love, strength, and resourcefulness, they survived near starvation, beatings, separation and much more, including:
- The German invasion of Poland
- Erwin's imprisonment in a work camp
- Being forced to build a labor camp
- Erwin barely surviving the Belitz work camp
- The Sosnowice ghetto; living in an attic
- Hiding in a basement
- The house getting bombed
- Surviving the long, difficult journey to the United States in April 1949 on the ship called **Haan**

What follows is a memoir of Hilda's first hand account of her experiences during Nazi Germany.

Hilda Thieberger; "to Erwin, with love"
by Herman Taube, from Between the Shadows

You're two minutes in her home and Hilda is already dancing around you
with a platter of food, cookies, drinks.
You set foot on her doorstep, touch her cheek with a friendly kiss,
and you feel at home at once.
Sit with Hilda for five minutes, and you're back four decades,
in fourteen concentration camps.
She is like the pelican who, according to legend, tears open its breast to
feed the young
with its own blood in times of hunger…
Hilda broke all Nazi rules, walked over forbidden borders
to find food to sustain her child.
Her home is full of pictures of her grandchildren
and the artwork of her husband.
She loves the present, but always thinks of the past…
the agonies of her tormented family,
ravaged by the Nazis.
There is an abundance of love,
striking humbleness in Hilda.
Like her Erwin, she carries no grudge,
no hatred for anyone.
There is grandeur in her smile after so many years…
the constant looking back to the extinct past,
combined with the will to live and love
is the secret to Hilda's survival!

From *Between the Shadows,* a collection of poetry by
Herman Taube, December 28, 1979
*Herman Taube, Holocaust survivor, authored 20 books of poetry and fiction,
taught at the University of Maryland and American University, and lectured
widely on Yiddish Literature and the Holocaust.*

1917 - 1929: Childhood

As a child, I lived with my mother, Rosa Gross, and my father, Julius Goldberger. My mother had five children, but two died before I was born. My brother Eric was one year younger than me, and my sister, Anna, was six years younger. Anna was sent to the town of Auschwitz, Poland, from Berlin to live with our grandfather when the war started, after the death of our father, when she was six years old. She did not survive. I feel guilty because when we were kids, I always pushed her away because she was younger and I didn't want her bothering me. As children, we climbed trees and were outside a lot with our friends. My mother never worked. I didn't see my father much. He worked as a sheet metal man and a firefighter, and he prayed every morning. There were two synagogues in Teschen; one was more religious than the other. My parents wanted us to be good people.

My grandparents lived in Cameron Elgot, Czechoslovakia, and we spoke German at home and in school.

Our family was considered middle class, because we had our own house in the suburbs, with two tenants. We didn't have much, but our extended family visited frequently. We slept in the same room with our parents, not like today, where every child has their own room. Six days a week, we walked about an hour to school, and then walked back home for the two hour lunch break. Many farmers lived in Teschen.

My mother, Rosa, was devoted to the Jewish life and to our family. She was close to both the Jewish and non-Jewish population, so whenever anyone needed food or any other assistance, my mother always helped. She was a very giving person, and everyone knew her. My mother often said, "When someone throws you a stone, throw back a piece of bread." She died at the age of 37, from an infection on her lip, when I was 12 years old. A year later, my father remarried because he needed help with us kids. My brother and sister went to Berlin but I stayed with my father. My parents were religious but not fanatic. They attended synagogue on holidays and kept a kosher home.

To make a living, many people had a trade, although some had stores. Everyone knew each other and helped each other.

My father worked in sheet metal, mostly roofing. He didn't have a car, so he hired horses and a wagon to transport roofing materials to a house, while he rode alongside on his bike.

The Town, Schooling, and The People
In those days, we attended school for eight years, and then learned a trade. When I finished high school, at the age of 15, I was supposed to go to trade school to learn dress-making for three more years, but I only attended for one year because my father died.

Teschen was divided by a river called the Orzo. Czechoslovakia was on one side, Poland on the other. We could cross the border freely, but had to show our papers to the border guards, and pay duty on things we bought.

About one third of the population was Jewish, but we didn't feel any differences between us and the non-Jewish families until Hitler came. As a child, I do not remember any anti-semitic incidents.

I attended a Catholic school. The nuns and other children treated us well. Eighteen out of 32 kids in my class were Jewish. The boys and girls studied together, but it was mostly girls.

When I was a young girl we had no lights or electricity, and we used a pump in the garden to get water. Because my parents died early, I wasn't involved with many organizations, but I did belong to Maccabi (Jewish Olympics.) I did gymnastics twice a week, so I was very strong. I also did a lot of handiwork. I made embroidery and gave them to my family as gifts. Later, I learned how to sew clothing, and became a dressmaker. I didn't know it at the time, but my sewing skills saved my life during the war.

When I was 12, I danced in a theater. Three of the best girls performed in a show, and we traveled around to different theaters. Everybody was friendly and we easily crossed back and forth over the borders.

Clothing

We wore the same clothes every day, except we had one special outfit for Sunday and holidays, and one for Shabbat *(a festive day when Jews exercise their freedom from the regular labors of everyday life, offering an opportunity to contemplate the spiritual aspects of life and spend time with family.)* Once a week we had a bath, but since there was no running water, we warmed the water on the stove and took turns in the bathtub. By the time the youngest child got into the tub, the water was pretty dirty.

1929 - 1932: Teen Years

For a while, I stayed with my step mother, Hermina Thieberger, who also happened to be my husband's sister. My husband had nine siblings, and she was one of the oldest. She was a widow and had a little store where I helped out. One day we had a fight so I left and worked in another store, which was much better for me.

I lived with the owners of the store. I worked very hard and they were good to me. Eventually, my stepmother came after me, very upset. She cried, "Why did you run away from me? I didn't mean what I said." She apologized, and made me go back to her store. So I left the good place and went back there.

My stepmother had moved from Teschen to Katovitz. [*capital city of the Silesian Voivodeship in southern Poland and the central city of the Upper Silesian metropolitan area.*] Eventually, we moved closer to Belitz, our home town, in Poland.

I cried a lot when I went back to work with my stepmother, because she made me miserable. She often fought with her sisters, and I always ended up being in the middle. I thought to myself, "Why am I here? There is too much aggravation. I will leave here, and learn how to sew."

So I went back to my hometown of Teschen and an older lady friend took me in. I lived with her and spent time with another woman every day learning how to sew dresses. This was in the early 1930's. My father died in 1928, so this was probably around 1932. When my mother died in 1925, I was thrown around from one place to another. I sang in a choir in the synagogue in my hometown, Teschen, and had many friends there.

We didn't notice ani-Jewish issues yet. My family was connected with big companies and we didn't have any problems. My brother learned to be a furrier in Germany. When the Nazi's came, he was beaten up on the street by some young men. They used to be friends, but when Hitler came and the friends found out he was Jewish, they told him "You should go back to Czechoslovakia, that's where you belong, we cannot protect you anymore." One time they hit him with a stick and broke his hand. He went back to Czechoslovakia and stayed for two years. He had a job as a furrier, but was required to join the Czech army. Then, On March 12, 1938, Hitler invaded Austria.

1932 - 1935: Belitz, Poland

My husband and I were married in Selazia, Poland. Everyone spoke German, and the schools were German. My husband was born in Germany but his parents moved to Poland when he was one year old. There were many Jews in Belitz. Most of the store owners were Jewish.

Customers came from the mountains once a week. It was a beautiful mountain city, called Klein Paris (small Paris), where Czechoslovakia, Germany and Poland intersected.

My husband was very smart, and could fix anything. My brother-in-law was also a very smart, self-educated man. He could speak, read and write in eight languages. He knew the five books of Moses. We were all Zionists. *[Zionists support a homeland for the Jewish people in the land of Israel.]*

I attended a few Zionist meetings because I always wanted to go to Israel, especially after I lost my parents. One of the boys I knew went on a hashada *[a training course for learning Hebrew and agriculture for would-be immigrants to Palestine, usually conducted in Europe but sometimes done upon arrival in Palestine.]*

I wanted to go very badly but my brother lived near me, and I didn't want to leave him, so I didn't go.

1935 - 1937: Marriage/family

In 1935 I got married in Belitz. We bought a little grocery store, and then I got pregnant, but my husband had to leave to join the Polish army, so he wasn't there most of the time. It was very challenging to run the store alone, and pregnant.

My daughter Renee was born in Belitz in 1937. When she was four months old there was a big revolution in Belitz.

A drunk man got into a fight with a Jewish restaurant owner, and the violence spread quickly. Every Jewish store was damaged by the Polish people. We lost everything, and decided it was time to run away.

Until that time, we hadn't experienced anti-semitic problems, but we still had a hard time. We were a young couple, didn't have much money, and were just starting out. The other stores had been there for years and could afford to buy and sell items cheaper than us. People mostly came for flour and sugar, so there wasn't much profit, but we had even less customers because we could not match the other stores prices. They could afford to lower the price on a few items to draw people into the store, and raise the prices on other things to make more profit.

After the riots, in the fall of 1937, we decided to leave. My sister-in-law gave us some space in her store, so my husband opened a bicycle shop. He bought bicycle parts wholesale, put them together, and sold the finished bikes. It was a great location for a bike store, because the trains stopped there, from Krakow, Katovitz, and Belitz. Every day, 150 to 200 men got off the trains, with their bikes, and walked through the town. Some of the men dropped off their old broken bicycles, and Erwin loaned them another one to take to work. When they came back in the evening, their bikes were fixed. People knew him before he had the store. He was well liked because he was a good man, and did a good job.

There were four main families in that town; Gichners, Thiebergers, Heshlovitz and Leflers. We didn't feel any difference at this point, in 1937. My husband worked with the bicycles in the store with his sister and he was starting to build a good business.

My daughter Renee was learning how to walk. She was so cute, and was such a good baby.

Although we were doing ok, we were aware that the Jews in Germany were losing their businesses and we heard rumors of other bad things happening. We heard that my grandparents lost everything.

We also heard about Kristallnacht in 1938 *[The Night of Broken Glass occurred on November 9 & 10, 1938. Nazi leaders unleashed a series of pogroms (violent riots incited with the aim of massacring or expelling an ethnic or religious group) against the Jewish population in Germany and incorporated territories. This event came to be called Kristallnacht because of the shattered glass that littered the streets after the vandalism and destruction of Jewish-owned businesses, synagogues, and homes]* We knew bad things were going on, and everyone was afraid to go in the street. No one had anything anymore, so they were just sitting home.

Although we could feel things changing, we felt safe because it was a friendly city. Everyone said hello. But, everything changed when the Germans came on **Sept. 1, 1939**.

1939: The German Invasion

By this time, the Germans were in Czechoslovakia, which was about one hour from the border by train.

Everyone knew they were coming, so we started mobilizing. I had a lot of Jewish items in my house because my grandfather was very religious and since I was the oldest in the family, I got everything, including his leather-bound books. I had wedding gifts too, like silverware and candlesticks. So when we heard that the Polish soldiers were preparing to make an appeal, we quickly built a bunker in our house to hide the special items and store some food. The walls were made of wood, so we hired two men to lift up the panels and make a hole in the wall, and then cover it up. We hid the treasures in the bunker and thought they would be safe from the Germans. We were wrong.

Close call with death

I will never forget the day the Germans invaded us, on Sept 1, 1939. We lived on the second floor of the house, so we could see and hear the German fighters flying over us. Sept. 1 was a Friday, and I usually baked a chicken, a turkey or a goose, and every week, the bakery across the street baked a challah for me.

But this was not a typical Friday. At 6:00 in the morning, when we heard the planes, we wondered what would happen next. We had no idea they would come so fast. At 10:00 I was about to get my challah from the bakery, but the Polish police came and said they were leaving because they saw fire in the distance, and would not be able to protect us from the

Germans. We knew that if we stayed, we would be killed. They said, "If you can go, go."

In those days, there were no strollers, so we put Renee, who was 18 months old, on a pillow in a wagon. I packed up the unbaked challah and the raw goose in a suitcase and added it to the wagon. My husband took four bicycles from the store. One for him, our maid and two boys from the store. Everyone got a bicycle, and we ran away. We were on the road for 11 days and nights. I lost Renee twice because everybody was running. It was chaos.

Both Jews and Polish people were running away. We had to leave everything behind. They were burning the houses. We went to Katovittz, then to Krakow, and wherever we went, they said we shouldn't stay because in the morning there will be a big fight, so we kept running, hoping they wouldn't catch up to us. Eventually, they did. We were so sick from all the running. On the way, my husband was attacked three times by Polish soldiers, because they wanted to take his bike away. We slept wherever we could. When we were so tired we couldn't walk anymore, we'd stop right there on the road, and try to sleep.

One day I lost Renee in the crowd, and crawled on my hands and knees to look for her. I was terrified that I wouldn't find her, but I did. The situation was unbelievable.

We all tried to stay together. My maid, my sister-in-law's maid, the two boys from the store, my child, my husband and me. The boys from the store weren't Jewish, but they were close to us, like family. When my husband went into the army they stayed in the store and protected me, and helped whenever they could.

At night, in the dark, we saw flames in the distance. It was terrifying. After ten days of walking, a woman who lived nearby said we could stay with her. Renee was crying the whole way, because she lost her pacifier.

Erwin was sick, so we were so grateful, and stayed with that woman for three days. When he started to feel better, we decided to go back home. We were afraid to go back, but we couldn't stay there either. Even though the Germans had passed us, we feared they might come back and kill us, so we figured why not try and go home.

We hired a man and some horses to take us back so we didn't have to walk all that way again. Before we left, my sister-in-law asked if they had eggs or other food we could take because we assumed all the food would be gone. They gave us some eggs, and we were so grateful, but it was very hot and they almost cooked inside the shell, so we couldn't eat them, but we put them to use. We boiled the eggs and fed them to the baby chickens. I wish we had cooked all of the eggs, but we left a few raw eggs in the box for some reason. I'll come back to that later.

We came home around Sept 15th. My brother, Eric, and my brother-in-law, Max, came back too. He wanted to observe Yom Kippur in a nearby village, with the whole family, but my husband didn't want to leave me and Renee alone, so he didn't go, but everyone else went on their bikes.

On Yom Kippur morning, at 4:00 AM, we heard a knock on the door. We got out of bed, and discovered 25 young German men with armbands and black coats standing outside of the house. They took my husband outside, as he was the only man in the house. They took him to the section of the house where the other men had built the bunker. They knew it was there, because the men who built it told them, but they didn't know the exact location. My husband said he didn't know anything about it, but they kept hitting him to make him talk. Eventually they found the hiding spot and took everything out; the sardines and other canned food, my good dishes, and other household items. Only the food was important, because we were afraid we might get stuck without food and starve to death.

They also went into the room where we had dances and found papers and a hunting gun. We were supposed to turn all guns in to the Germans but we didn't think we had to turn in that one because it was a hunting gun. A customer left it as payment for a bike because he had no money.

When they found the gun, the Germans started yelling, "The Jew has a gun, the Jew has a gun!" Then they found the extra rotten eggs I mentioned earlier. They shoved my husband into the corner, facing the wall, and threw all the eggs at his head. He was standing in that corner all day. The Germans sat around and ate all the food, and threw the empty cans at my husband. Then they loaded the other items onto the truck, and forced my husband into the truck as well.

While all this was happening, I was upstairs in the bedroom with my daughter Renee. When they took everything, I was upset but there was nothing I could do. When I saw them force my husband on the truck, I ran to the window with Renee in my arms and I screamed in German; "He didn't do anything to anybody, why are you taking my husband? Let him go!" One of the German boys pointed a gun at us and said "If you don't move away from the window, I will shoot you!" I barely heard him, because I was so upset and nervous.

What happened next was unbelievable. To this day I don't know if the wind moved me or I moved myself or God moved me, but I moved away just as four shots came through the window and went through the ceiling. If I didn't move, I would be dead with my daughter by that window. I swear I don't remember if I moved myself or what made me move, as I was so upset that they were taking my husband away.

We had no idea where they took him, or if he was still alive. Someone told us they saw people digging graves on the side of the road, and then the Germans shot everyone from a truck and pushed them into the grave. We didn't know if my husband was amongst them.

Every day we had a little bit of news about what was going on in the towns around us, and after a while we were relieved to find out that my husband was alive. He was in a regular jail in Belitz, about two and a half hours away by foot. Our neighbors' husband was there as well, because he was accused of stealing a hat. The Germans made up excuses to arrest people, for practically nothing. The wife came to my house and said "My husband is in the same jail with your husband. We are allowed to bring them clothes." So we gathered some clothes and walked two and a half hours to the jail in Belitz. When we arrived, they said we could bring him clean clothes every week, and they would give me his dirty clothes to wash. I wasn't allowed to see him, so I wasn't sure if he was there, but the next time we went, there was a package wrapped in newspaper, and inside was his dirty underwear and undershirt along with a note in his handwriting that said "Next time you come, please send a picture of you and Renee." So the following week I brought a picture and put some money in the package. He said his brother was in jail too, but we didn't know how long he was there or how he got there.

Three months later, my brother-in-law came back.

I screamed, "Where is Erwin? We heard you were together." He told us that they were not in the same cell. He was in the basement, and they beat him and he screamed all night as water dripped on him from the ceiling. In the morning they brought him up to the single cell where my husband was, along with eleven other men. Because they were so crammed together in that little cell, when they tried to sleep, if one of them moved, the others had to move too. Later, my husband said he heard the screaming in the basement, and although the voice was familiar, he had no idea it was his brother. My husband was a little bit better off than some of the others because he had a job washing the big pots in the kitchen.

My brother-in-law explained how he ended up coming home but my husband was still in jail. He said, "One morning, they called out all the names on a list. Erwin was on the list, but I wasn't. They told the men to take whatever they had because they were going home. I started to cry, because I was being left behind, but Erwin said to me; 'Don't cry, I'll leave you everything that I have, including the money Hilda sent me, and I will do everything in my power to get you out.' Twenty minutes later, they came back and told me to go to the office. When I got there, I saw a truck filled with men, including Erwin. They told me to go home. The truck drove away, but I didn't know where they were going. So I came home, but Erwin was taken somewhere else on that truck."

Within three days, my brother-in-law had to register with the Jewish Community Center (JCC) in Belitz because they were sending people to make houses on the Russian border.

One day I overheard my brother-in-law talking to his wife. They were speaking very low but I heard him mention my husband's name. He said a man from our street ran away from a prison in Czechoslovakia and my husband was with him, and they went into hiding with my father-in-law. He heard that my husband looked terrible; he was so beaten up that he was not recognizable.

I didn't believe him; I thought it was only a story. But after three months, the man from our street came back. Since I lived close to the road, he had to walk by my house on the way to his house, so I confronted him. I said, "Where is my husband?"
He replied, "I can't tell you much. They called the names alphabetically. My name is Heshlovitz, and they asked if I am able to walk and I said yes so they let me go, and I figured your husband would be called later."
I pleaded with him to come into my house and tell me more but he said he could not talk.

"I have to register at the JCC because in three days we will go to the Russian border. I cannot come upstairs to your house because I am full of lice, and I don't want to infect your home, and I have to go home." But I begged him. "Mr. Heshlovitz, please come and tell me. I need to know what happened." He said Erwin was very sick, but he was coming home and should be back in two or three days. I will never forget the days waiting. After three days, my sister-in-law went to Belitz, and she asked me what I needed form the city, and I said, "Just my husband."

1939: Erwin Comes Home

On his way back, Erwin registered at the Jewish Community Center, and then continued waking home. It was normally a two hour walk, but took much longer because he was in such bad shape. When he finally walked into the house, no one recognized him, except the dog. His own mother didn't recognize him. He was so beaten up; he couldn't sit, he couldn't lie down, he was full of lice and could barely talk. He told me that he and a few other men were sitting by a round oven, and someone pushed him towards the oven, so he got burned. He was very beaten up, and had no meat on his body.

Later, I found out more details. Of the 50 people that were loaded onto the truck, only four were still alive. After driving for a while, they told everyone to get off the truck. There was a large table with heavy legs in a room with benches on either side for the SS to sit. One by one the men were forced to go into the room and lie down on the table. When it was my husband's turn, he said, the floor was covered with blood.

When he walked into the room, they put a potato sack over his head, tied his hands together, and forced him to lie down on the table. One of the men pulled his hands up above his head, and another man beat him. They forced him to count. I have a letter from a Polish man who was there and saw the whole thing. We needed the letter to prove what happened after the war. In the letter, he described everything, including how he found my husband barely alive.

My husband said he began to count but he doesn't remember how far, because he lost consciousness. When he woke up they removed the sack, and one man sat on his head so he couldn't move. His hands were still tied. Then they dumped a pan of water over his head. Although he was awake, didn't feel anything. He was in and out of consciousness and felt no pain. When the torture was over, they forced my husband and the other men to run away, even though they could barely walk. They probably figured they would never make it back home alive because of the beatings.

The torture took place in an old sugar factory, in Stokovitz, Czechoslovakia. Many people died there.

When my husband felt a little better, he found out that his brother-in-law was killed three days before. His brother-in-law was also beaten, but Mr. Herschlovitz, who was also with them, did not get a beating at first. Somehow he slept through it all. Eventually the Germans found out that he avoided the beatings, so they beat him up and they broke his nose. He was still able to go to work, and he got some milk for my husband, but he couldn't swallow, and could barely move, because of how beat up he was. He had to lie on his stomach because his back was so sore from the beatings. The Polish men slept on the floor; the Jewish men and the priests were up on a platform. They treated the priests exactly like Jews.

Another man from Krakow, named Aaron, was with them. He appeared to be a crazy man, and was in an institution before the Germans came, but the Germans let everyone out of the asylum, and brought them to the old sugar factory.

Every morning, when the SS men came into the factory, they said, "Aaron, climb up the ladder and yell 'The Jews are the **worst** people in the world.'" He did what he was told, and then the Germans threw him a piece of bread as a reward. Every day, they did the same thing. One day, instead of the usual phrase, he yelled, "The Jews are the **chosen** people of the world!" and the SS man screamed, "What did you say? You made a mistake, say what you are supposed to say!" but he repeated the same thing; "The Jews are the **chosen** people of the world!" They said, "Aaron, come down here." Then they beat him. He had to stand there as they hit him, and then they said, "Go back up the ladder and say 'The Jews are the **worst** people in the world'" but still, he said the other phrase, "The Jews are the **chosen** people." They kept beating him but he refused to say what they demanded, and eventually he could no longer speak. It turned out that this man, Aaron, took care of my husband the whole time. So I guess he wasn't so crazy in the head after all.

Aaron used his own urine to wash my husband's wounds. His injuries were so severe that even after three months, he was still very sore. It's a miracle that he survived, especially under those terrible conditions, and with no medical care.

When they started to let people go, they ran down the alphabet starting with "A", and on the first day, they got to the letter "H", so Mr. Herschlovitz was allowed to leave. The next day, they were supposed to keep going with the alphabet, but they decided to start with "Z" and since my husband's last name started with "T", he was one of the first to be let go on the second day. They asked if he could walk, and he said yes, so they let him go. If he had said no, he never would have come home. We found out later that Mr. Herschlovitz was killed.

When he first came home he wasn't able to sit, and he couldn't tell me what happened. Luckily my brother-in-law was there, so he washed and cleaned my husband but they didn't let me go into the room because they didn't want me to see how bad his injuries were. The Germans told him that if he said one word about what happened, he would be killed. So he was afraid to talk. A few days later, he registered at the JCC and they told him, "Within three days, you must bring your wife and your child here and we will send you to Brzezinka (Selasia, Poland.)"

1940: Auschwitz, Poland

Since my husband was still so weak, we had to try to escape, otherwise, he would likely be killed because he could not keep up with the others. Somehow we got papers, and smuggled ourselves to the town of Auschwitz, Poland, because there was a river there and we could cross to the other side.

When God wants to save you, he does. We went to the town of Auschwitz, Poland. The Jews had a ghetto there; this was not where the ovens were. This was in 1939. I knocked on every door for many days trying to find a place to stay with my child and my husband, but no one would let us in because they saw how sick my husband was, and they were afraid he would die in their home.

Finally, a woman let us in. She lived with her daughter, and they had a spare room. She asked how she could help us. I told her that my husband was very sick from being in a work camp, and could not walk anymore. She let us stay in her only bedroom, and she and her daughter stayed in the kitchen or another small room she had. Her name was Mrs. Becker.

She helped us so much. For example, she cooked a lot of chicken soup for my husband. Even so, it took months for my husband to heal. When he felt better, he went to work fixing typewriters in an office. But in the spring, all the Jewish people had to leave and go to the Russian border to build houses for families. At the time, my aunt was in Krakow, and she gave us the name of someone who had an extra flat in their house with four rooms. We went there and rented the flat. Me and my husband, my father-in-law and my daughter were in one room together. His three sisters were in the other room.

It was hard to communicate but we found ways. People knew us. We got around on bicycles or horses; there were no cars. There were good people and bad people. We were afraid of the bad people, and it was hard to know who to trust. For example, a German man offered to give my husband his passport so we could get away, but we weren't sure we could trust him. My husband always had good jobs because he was very handy.

When we were in Auschwitz, he wanted to go to work. He went to the Jewish Community Center and fixed broken typewriters for the Germans. Even though he had no experience fixing typewriters, he figured it out, just like when I was in the lager *[forced labor camp]* sewing men's uniforms. I knew how to sew dresses but not uniforms. They gave me the material, and even though I had never done that before, somehow I figured it out. If you asked me to do that today, I don't think I could do it again.

Before the war, I got my certificate for sewing. I learned how to sew in one place, and then went to another location to show what I learned. I had to make the pattern and cut it and sew it by myself and show it to the boss. It had to be perfect. They taught me how to make women's clothes, but others were learning how to make men's clothes, so I saw how they made jackets, especially the collar. Maybe that's how I figured out how to make the uniforms. You have to make it a specific way, otherwise it doesn't stay firm. It took me longer than the others to learn how to sew. Often, when I tried to make a piece of clothing, it wasn't done right, and I had to take it apart and try again and again until I got it right.

As long as we served a purpose, we had a better chance of survival. We lived in the Ghetto of Auschwitz, and Germans and Polish people lived on the outskirts. Even if they weren't born in Germany, people made themselves German. We had to stay in the Ghetto; we were not allowed to leave. My grandfather was born in the town of Auschwitz, Poland. Before the war, it was a religious city.

This is when we found out that they were building the gas chambers and crematoria.

The SS picked people from the JCC and hired men for the day. They took them outside of the lager to work.

The soldiers lived in the barracks, in the army camp, where they were building the ovens. The Jews were forced to work there, including my brother Eric. It was a very difficult life, but everyone pitched in and we got through. We lived in a small apartment with my mother-in-law and two sisters and my sister's husband. We all shared a kitchen.

Eventually my aunt came to live with us, all in the same room.

The SS told my husband that if he went to work, they would protect me and my daughter. So, he went to work. His brother-in-law and many others went too.

They worked at a clothing factory in Belitz making material for men's and women's suits. The head of the ghetto there respected my husband and let him do special work. About thirty people lived in the ghetto including carpenters, electricians, and other tradesmen. Everyone had a trade, so we were somewhat protected from the extermination camps since we were useful to the Germans.

We lived in fear of death every day. We were also frightened they would separate us; which they did for a while, when my husband had to go to a work camp. Luckily, the man in charge was not an SS man. He was a good boss compared to some of the others, and allowed the men to visit their families. During this time, my mother-in-law passed away from a heart attack.

Once they finished building the crematoria, (ovens) everyone had to leave Auschwitz, so we packed up our things and they moved us to another ghetto called Bedzin, in **1941**. I moved there with my daughter and my aunt and cousin. We had a very hard time there.

1941: Bedzin

In the morning, we packed up everything we had, including our beds, and piled into the freight cars on the train. We didn't know where we were going.

We ended up in Bedzin. It was a dirty city. The people who lived there were forced to find room for us in their homes, because there was no place else for us to go. They came to the train station and chose who would live in their homes. They were not happy about this, because they were forced to give up rooms in their homes for us.

We had many difficulties during this time. When we departed the train, the German soldiers separated the men from the women and children, and then separated the children from their mothers. The children were taken away and killed. Somehow I found out ahead of time, so when we got off the train, I told Renee to hide under my skirt, and when I walked, to walk with me, so she would not be seen. She did what I told her, and her life was spared.

My aunt got very sick on the train, so they took her out on a stretcher, and put her on a pile of straw at the train station. Because she was so ill, we sat there for three days. Nobody wanted to take us in. My aunt, my cousin and I thought we would all die there. Somehow, I got in touch with my husband, who was still at the work camp, to let him know what was going on, and if there was anything he could do to help. The lieutenant in charge of the work camp liked my husband and relied on him because he was such a good worker, so the lieutenant sent a letter to the JCC, saying that they better find a place for us to live quickly, because he needed his best worker to focus on working and not worry about his family. He said they would be punished if they didn't find a place for us to live. My husband brought the letter to the JCC and then came to see us.

Right away, a woman showed up and said she had a room for us in her attic. She took us to her house, and guided us to wooden steps that lead up to a tiny attic room. There was another woman, Mrs. Bernstein, living in the attic, but she wasn't there when we arrived. Her bed was in the corner.

At first, we had nowhere to sleep because we didn't have our furniture yet. The furniture was being delivered on the sidewalks, but everything was covered in snow, so it was hard to figure out which furniture was ours. I looked for days and days, and finally figured it out. By then, my aunt was feeling much better. She was very clean and washed the floor every day in the attic. It was filthy, and full of bedbugs. One time, I touched the table and there were so many bugs, they scattered like ants. It was horrible. My aunt tried to get rid of the bugs by cleaning and scrubbing the room, and smeared onion everywhere because that was supposed to keep them away. We hardly got any sleep because of the bugs.

To keep myself busy and help the family, I knitted sweaters using wool that people brought to me. They sometimes brought peas or beans or potatoes to pay me for the sweaters so we had something to eat, and my husband usually brought some food when he visited. He always stopped in the city to see his father, because his mother had already died.

When the other woman who lived in the attic room, Mrs. Bernstein, came back, she never let anyone near her bed, because she peed in her bed every night, and it smelled horrible, because it never dried out. We didn't know right away why it smelled so bad, but then we figured it out.

She made us miserable, and complained about us all the time. The Jewish police came and wanted to throw us out of the apartment because of her complaints. I went back to the JCC and explained that we were keeping the room clean, and we didn't understand why she wanted to kick us out. So, they let us stay.

When my husband came to visit I begged him to get us out of there. We hardly had any food because when I went to the food distribution building with my ration card, usually nothing was left. The people who lived in the city pushed themselves forward with their sticks, screaming that we should go to the back of the line. Since they all knew each other and we were strangers, we were the ones who ended up with no food.

I sent my husband many letters and messages, begging him to get us out of there. My daughter had nothing to eat; she was practically starving to death. Eventually, he took Renee to a lager where she stayed with a Jewish family, the Rosenthals.

When the Germans threw the Jewish families out of their apartments in Belitz, including their furniture, everything from the apartments ended up in the lager where we were staying. The furniture and lamps and other useful items were repaired and placed into various apartments where the Germans were staying. Many houses were bombed out. The younger boys brought the furniture to where we were using a wagon. The three girls cooked for the 30 boys. I was a dressmaker.

This was in 1942 I think. We were there for two years. We had a little room with two beds and a sewing machine. My husband was the foreman for the other boys. They fixed up the furniture that was brought in. He was paid 50 cents a day for that work. I didn't get paid for the sewing work I did.

During this time, my daughter Renee was back with us, and we were a little better off regarding food. Sometimes the boys and my husband went into town to get the furniture and since my husband used to live there, he knew people, so he could organize food for us. The gardeners gave him vegetables, and the fishermen gave him fish. Once a month, the lieutenant received a food ration paper and made a copy somehow. He took one copy to one butcher, and another copy to another butcher so he got double food rations. Once in a while, when they had to put down an injured horse, we had horse meat. Nothing was wasted. We also got double vegetable rations from the farmers, and a little bit of fruit.

Ours wasn't the only lager that had trades. There were 50 smaller lagers within the larger neighborhood, and each had about 20 people. We had to be very careful about what we said, because if we said anything bad about the Germans, we could be killed. Polish people also lived in the lagers because they were kicked out of their homes when the Germans came.

The lieutenant was in charge of all 50 lagers. Once or twice a month he hopped onto his motorcycle and went from one lager to another. My husband always went with him because he knew how to fix the motorcycle if anything went wrong. He wasn't a trained mechanic, but somehow he figured it out. For example, he helped reconfigure the trucks to run on wood instead of gas. He tried to be useful to the Germans because it was the only way to stay alive.

While I was there, I sewed a lot, mostly fixing pants and mending uniforms. Although we had a front yard, I never went out because I was always upstairs working. Wooden steps led up to the room, and once in a while the policemen assigned to guard us came upstairs to inspect the lager and make sure everything was ok. Whenever I heard them coming up the wooden steps, I quickly hid Renee under the bed or under the pile of dirty laundry in the corner because there were no children allowed in the lagers. If they found her, they would take her away and she would likely be killed.

When they came in the evening I hid her under the feather covers because they were fluffy and you couldn't see her if she stayed perfectly still. But one time I almost killed her by suffocation because the soldiers stayed for so long, and she could hardly breathe.

The "good" lieutenant knew about Renee, but he liked my husband so much he turned the other cheek. He said, "I know nothing about it. Just take care of her. But if anything happens, I can't cover for you." If the soldiers knew about her, they didn't say anything because they were under the lieutenant and they followed his lead.

Eventually, Glugosh, the good lieutenant, was thrown out because his superiors found out how good he treated us. They brought in an SS man, Mr. Heinz Kollup, also called a Hauptsturmführer *[a Nazi Party paramilitary rank used in several Nazi organizations such as the SS, NSKK and the NSFK. The rank of Hauptsturmführer was a mid-level commander and had equivalent seniority to a captain (Hauptmann) in the German Army]* Mr. Kollup was a younger man, and liked to drink, so they made whiskey, and whenever someone found a bottle of whiskey they brought it to him.

Mr. Glugosh told Mr. Kollup that my husband was very smart and could do anything and was the best worker, so Mr. Kollup was also good to my husband. Sometimes the butcher gave my husband an extra piece of meat because he knew him from before the war.

Often, Mr. Kollup would come to my room for a visit, so I had to hide Renee. Sometimes this was very difficult because she sat on the potty a lot, due to frequent stomach aches. In our attic room, a little door opened into a smaller room for storing books and other items, so sometimes she had to sit there while Mr. Kollup was in the room. One time, he came up to visit and was sitting for what seemed like hours, talking and talking, and Renee was hiding in that little room, and after a while, she started to knock on the other side of the door. He was already drunk but he heard the knocking and asked, "What was that sound?" I tried to make other noises to cover up her knocks and also to let her know I heard her and I didn't forget about her.

Eventually we didn't have a choice, and we had to tell him about Renee. He said "Why are you afraid? Bring her out. I will not do anything to her, I have a child too, my son is in the army." So I brought her out from the little room and now our secret was out. We tried to stay on his good side by bringing him things like food or whiskey.

One day, out of the blue, we were told to pack up our belongings because they were taking us to Selazia, Germany, to work. My brother was already there, and somehow he sent my husband a message. "Don't take Hilda and Renee to the German lager in Selazia. They will be taken to Auschwitz right away and killed."

At this time, we didn't know much about what was happening in Auschwitz. We knew the ghetto was segregated. There was only one door in, and no door out. I can't remember if I knew about the gassing at this point in time.

Once we heard this news, my husband told the SS man that he did not want his wife and child to go to the German work camps. He said "Why not? I am going with you too." Although we had a bit of freedom where we were, the German lagers were more restrictive. They put the Jews to work, clearing out forest to make room for the autobahn, or working in the factories. There were no children there at all. We also heard stories about Polish people being hanged because they didn't have their papers, and the Jews were forced to watch. My husband didn't know what to do. He didn't want me and Renee to go to Germany because we would likely be killed.

Around this time, someone brought a large safe to the lager. The Germans suspected it might contain something valuable, but they didn't have the keys to the safe. Since my husband was a mechanic, the SS men forced him to try and open the safe. They watched him the whole time, so that if he opened it, he would not steal what was inside. My husband and another man spent days trying to open it. Eventually they figured it out, but they kept it quiet because they wanted to try and open it without the SS men watching and take some of the contents for themselves. They waited until night, when everyone was sleeping, to open it. There wasn't anything terribly valuable, except a few watches and other small items. They took a few things out of the safe and hid them, and then they opened the safe the next day in front of the SS man.

1943: Sewing to Survive in Bistra

In June of 1943, the SS men took all the Jewish and Polish men to Germany. We didn't know much about what was happening in Germany, we were just trying to survive day to day.

My husband told the SS man that I had a place to stay in town, because we were afraid to go to the German lager. Initially, he said we still needed to go, and he promised that he would protect us. But in the end, he let me and my daughter go. We stayed there for two more weeks, and my husband made arrangements with the butcher and the baker to help us with food. After two weeks, the SS man came looking for me. He wanted me to go with him to the new lager, but I said no, I wanted to stay where I was.

He asked about Renee, and then gave me a ticket for the train to go back to where we were before. Somehow, we ended up living in a barn with a kitchen attached to it. The family who lived in the main house worked for the SS. Again, I found a way to be useful. The wife of one of the SS men said I could do sewing at her villa. We were there for about a year.

The SS man who lived in the house was terrible. He had a high position with Hitler. We found out he had murdered some Polish people. But as bad as he was, his wife was ten times worse. Part of the reason they treated us so badly was the Germans were required to attend lectures, where they were fed propaganda and taught to hate the Jews. The woman of the house was in charge of a hat store in Germany, which had been owned by Jews and then was taken over by the Germans. When someone brought food to the store for the Jewish owner, who was not there anymore, she took it for herself.

After a while, she promised that we could move out of the shed and into an attic room in the house that was being fixed up. She told me to keep it a secret from the other ten Jews and Polish people living in the shed behind the house. I didn't interact with them very much since I spent the entire day cooking and sewing in the main house. They did everything for the SS man and his family, like brushing his shoes and washing clothes. I did much of the cooking. So although we were basically slaves, we were alive. This situation was common. Many small groups like this were scattered around, and an SS man was always in charge.

Renee and I slept in the shed while the attic room was being completed. We walked to the main house at 7:00 in the morning to bake bread, feed the dog, and bake a cake for her.

Another young girl worked there but she didn't know how to cook. After I finished cooking, I spent the rest of the day at the sewing machine. Renee sat in the kitchen, right next to the sewing room, by the window. When the farmers came to pick up the finished sewing projects, they would sometimes bring her a piece of salami, or a piece of bread, or butter, or an egg, or something. We were so grateful, because we had very little food.

The room still wasn't ready a week later, so I continued walking to the main house every morning, and then back to the shed in the evening. One day, the woman told me I could not bring my daughter with me anymore. She had to stay in the shed with a younger woman, who had an eight month old baby. Renee was four years old.

On the first day, when I tried to leave her behind, she cried and cried. Here's why.

A few weeks before, three girls were staying with us in the shed for a few days. Two of them were pregnant. They ran away from the German ghetto because they were not allowed to have babies. This was before we had to wear the striped uniforms. The girls were very nice to Renee, so she liked them. They took care of her while I was working at the woman's house all day.

They wanted to have their babies, so they told the SS man they had some gold hidden under their houses back in their hometown, near Sosnowitz. [*The Ghetto von Sosnowitz was a World War II ghetto set up by Nazi German authorities for Polish Jews in the Środula district of Sosnowiec in the Province of Upper Silesia. (wikipedia)*] They said, "If you let us have our babies, we will give you the gold. We promise to kill our babies as soon as they are born." Otherwise, they would be sent to Auschwitz.

He agreed and the next day, he took them to their homes. They dug up the gold and other valuables, and then he brought them back, but the next morning he called the police. They were taken away, and sent to Auschwitz to be killed. Renee saw everything and was very upset.

The SS man lied about why the girls got picked up. He said, "Those stupid girls told someone in their lager where they were going, so the police knew they were here, that's why they came and picked them up." Of course I did not believe him, I think he called the police on them. After that, my daughter was very scared and never wanted to leave my side.

The other woman who worked in the shed kitchen, with the baby, was very busy cooking and never had time to care for her baby. Whenever Renee was in the kitchen with them, the woman told Renee to go play with the baby, who was less than a year old. She scared her by saying, "If you don't play with the baby, your momma won't come back for you at the end of the day."

So I told Renee to stay in the lager and I would come back in the evening, but she was too afraid because of what the other woman said to her. She tried to follow me to the house sometimes, and I had to hit her so she would stay behind. It was terrible. I cried so much because I would never hit my child, but I had no other choice. I did not know what to do. I cried all day when I was sewing, my eyes were always puffy and swollen from all the crying. When I tried to leave in the morning, Renee grabbed onto my clothes, and promised she would be good if I took her with me. But I feared she would be taken away and killed if we did not obey the rules, so I had to leave her behind. Sometimes, when I came back after working all day, she was sleeping in the corner, all dirty, and I woke her up to wash her, and she begged to come with me the next day.

I asked the SS man when my husband would come back and he said "He is not coming back." So I had no place to go.

Mr. Libetsky, a close friend, ran away from another lager and came to our lager. He had Polish papers, so he had the freedom to go out and get food. He told the SS man he was Greek, not Jewish, and it was a mistake for him to be in the lager. He sat by the window and when he saw the SS man coming he hid in the hayloft.

And then, one day, my husband got in contact with me. He was in another lager, called Gleiwitz, with his brother and other members of his family. One of the SS men working in the lager with us was also from Gleiwitz *[a city in Upper Silesia, in southern Poland. The city is located in the Silesian Highlands, on the Kłodnica river (a tributary of the Oder). Wikipedia.]*

Not everyone was mean to us. Even though they were trained to hate the Jews, not everyone did. But they were afraid of each other. So, I took a chance and asked this man if he was going back to Gleiwitz, could he bring a letter to my husband?

He delivered the letter, and my husband wrote back. We had to try anything to help ourselves, because we knew our days were numbered and why not take a chance. We were desperate; we knew death was close.

Everyone knew my husband. He was working with 12 men. Every day they came out at 5:00 AM and went on the train to Blechhammer *[The* **Blechhammer** *area was the location of Nazi Germany chemical plants, prisoner of war (POW) camps, and forced labor camps. Wikipedia]* and in the evening they went back. My husband wanted to escape, but his two sisters and brother were in the lager too, so he was afraid that if he ran away, they would be killed because whenever anyone did something wrong, they were killed on the spot, or sent to Auschwitz.

This was December, 1944, and he could not take the chance to run away. I was miserable. Our living conditions were terrible. It was cold, and we had very little wood to make a fire, and very little food or water. We had to get water from the well. I shared a room with the woman who worked in the kitchen and her baby.

When I came back to the shed after working in the main house all day, it was always a mess. The other men living there did nothing. They said if I would sleep with them they would help me with the chores. I thought, to hell with you I will not sleep with anyone. I already have a good husband. So I did everything myself.

One evening I came home late. I washed Renee and put her to bed, and then washed myself and went to bed. Then, the meanest SS man came in. He stunk very badly. He ordered everyone out of bed, but he probably didn't know I had my daughter there. He said "Everyone get up and get dressed, they are coming to take you all to Auschwitz. Thieberger, get dressed." I said, "No, I am not getting dressed. You can shoot me here. I am not going anywhere. Shoot me here."

He went into the other room to see if the other boys were getting dressed. Tousha (the woman with the baby) got dressed and he kept insisting I get dressed because they are coming to take us all away and I kept saying no. Then he saw that everyone else was dressed except for me, and he said, "Go back to bed." I don't know why I didn't have a heart attack right there.

It was bad there, but it was worse in other places. Because I had a trade, I was able to work and tried to please everyone. I sat day and night by the sewing machine to get all the work done. If someone was coming the next day to pick up a dress, I stayed at the machine until it was done.

The SS woman also had me baking cakes, and bread for the dog. Sometimes, after I made the dough, I tore off a small piece and stuck it in my dress pocket. When I had to stay longer in the evening to finish work, the dough would start growing in my pocket, so I had to keep pushing at it so it would not be detected. Back in the lager there was a wood stove and an oven so I could bake the dough. So at least I had something for my child to eat.

One time the SS woman was walking behind me on the stairs, and I turned around and the dough fell out of my pocket and I was afraid to pick it up. I said it was for the dog. She believed me.

One day, the SS woman asked me to bring Renee to the house with me so she could play with and babysit her friend's son. Renee was around four or five, and he was two. In the evening when I picked her up, the mother gave me an egg as payment for the babysitting. I was so happy to have that egg because I had hardly any food to give my daughter.

Sometimes the people for whom I was sewing would bring some milk or bread or butter for Renee. One day I asked the SS woman if I could go get the milk from the farmer. So, in the evening she gave me the container and off I went. Sometimes it was far to go, but it was the only way to get milk for my daughter. On the way back from the farm I stopped at my lager and put some of the milk in a pot. Then I took the same amount of water and replaced the amount I took so she couldn't tell.

I was so happy that she was getting the egg. But then, one day, when she was playing with the boy and his toys, (Renee had no toys) she got distracted and the boy ran off near the street. His mother was very angry that she wasn't paying attention to him, so she was not allowed to babysit anymore. I was so upset because that meant no more eggs, so I spanked her but she really didn't do anything wrong. She was so young and didn't know any better. It was a bad time. Renee wanted to go back to play with the toys, because she never had any toys. But she was not allowed.

1943: New Year's Eve Escape

Around Christmas, 1943, the man who had the Polish papers, Mr. Lubetsky, said that everyone in the lager had to wear the uniforms with the stripes. I knew that once that happened, there would be no escape.

One of our friends went to Gleiwitz and saw Erwin, my husband, a few weeks before Christmas. He went to the factory where he was working, and he said "Can I speak to Mr. Learner?" He made up that name. And he didn't wait for an answer, he just went inside. The security man chased after him and said, "There is no one here by that name." But he was already inside. He saw my husband working under a truck, along with 12 other men. He said to my husband, "I am in contact with your wife in Bistra. After New Years they will make everyone wear striped uniforms, and there will be no way to escape once that happens. New Year's Eve is the best time to run away because all the Germans will be drunk."

He gave my husband some money, and they decided to try. A few days before New Year's eve, they asked a tailor to cut the cuffs on his pants so he could patch them on top of the yellow Jewish Star so they would not be noticed.

On New Year's Eve they escaped. It was very dark, so they helped each other climb over the fence. They didn't go to the station where they usually went. They walked on the sidewalk, and went to another station. My husband saw a policeman on the corner, so he went straight to the policeman to distract him while the other man bought the train tickets and asked what time it was. The policeman got annoyed and said, "Can't you see the clock on the wall?" But the plan worked.

His friend got the two tickets, but he mistakenly went through the gate with both tickets. When Erwin tried going through the gate, the ticket-taker asked, "Where is your ticket?" and my husband said, "That man has my ticket!" And he ran towards his friend. Just then a train pulled into the station and even though they didn't know which way it was going, they jumped on. Many drunk soldiers were on the train. They were singing, so my husband started singing with them in German to fit in. He found out they were going in the opposite direction from where they wanted to go, so they got off at the next station and caught the next train going in the right direction.

They bought new tickets and went to Katowice *[the capital city of the Silesian Voivodeship in southern Poland and the central city of the Upper Silesian metropolitan area. Wikipedia]* They arrived at 2:00 AM. I will never forget that day. It was snowing, and everyone was sleeping so no one saw them come in. He knocked on the door, and I was overjoyed to see him. For three weeks, he was in hiding, and no one knew he was there, but then they caught him because he fell asleep on the bed and one of the SS men came in. They knew who he was. So they called the SS man in charge and told him that Thieberger was here.

While this was going on, I was in the house working at the sewing machine. The SS man told me he had a big surprise for me. I acted dumb. He told me my husband was here, and I should go see him. I acted surprised. It turned out, they were happy he was there, because he had a lot of helpful skills. They put him to work right away; laying bricks around the house, fixing the car, and many other things.

1944: Escape to Belitz

We were there for four months. One day, when my husband and Mr. Lerner were working for the SS woman, she came outside and told my husband to leave right away because the Germans were coming in two hours to pick up everyone and take them to Auschwitz. She didn't care about the others but told us to disappear for two to three days. After they picked up the other people, she said we could come back and would be safe there. So my husband came home and we packed everything up.

My husband told everyone else, even though she said not to. Why should we be safe and not the others? Everyone ran away. We went back to Belitz, and my husband asked the butcher if we could hide there for a few days but he said no because SS men and policemen were always stopping by to get supplies and we might get caught. He said he could help with ration cards or whatever else we needed but they could not hide us. Then we asked the baker's wife and she also said no. We asked another friend, Alfred Goodman, to help us. He was hiding for a year because he had false papers.

Mr. Goodman was staying in a Polish woman's apartment sometimes, on the 4th floor, and he told us if we were in danger we should come there and hide. My husband was well known so we were afraid someone would recognize him, so we went to the apartment in the evening. The Polish maid knew we were coming and let us in. It was a very big apartment building where only very wealthy Jewish people lived before the war. Then the Germans took it over and lived there when the Jews were kicked out.

A German doctor lived there and the Polish woman was his maid, but the doctor wasn't there at the time, so we stayed with her in the doctor's apartment. Luckily, there were two entrances. Three or four days later, another Polish woman brought us food. Sometimes, Renee went to a farmer's house with the maid and brought back food. Another friend, Marisha, offered to take Renee for a few days to get her more food.

Mr. Goodman sometimes came to visit in the evening and we listened to the radio together. The apartment was split into two rooms; the doctor's office on one side, his living quarters on the other side. There was a room in-between with a thick glass door that you could not see through. A toilet was next to that room, and there was a bed, where we slept. Our friend, Mr. Lerner, was with us all the time. Renee was with the Polish woman, Marisha, for a few days. One night when we were listening to the radio, we heard heavy footsteps and we figured it was the Gestapo because they wore heavy boots. We turned off the radio. My husband hid under one bed, and our friend went under the other bed, and I think I went into the toilet to hide. Mr. Goodman was still out there. The SS men came into the apartment, and the maid had just prepared some jello or some food, and gave them each a little plate in the kitchen, and they asked, "Where is the partisan *[a person who was part of the communist-led anti-fascist resistance against Nazi Germany during WWII.]* who just came up to the apartment?"

Apparently, someone saw Mr. Lerner come up the steps and called the police. The maid tried to make up a story. She knocked on the glass door and said, "Alfred, someone wants to talk to you." We were all hiding, so he opened the door and went out. We locked the door, but they never tried to come into the room. They asked Alfred a bunch of questions about why he was there. The maid came into the room and begged us to run away so she didn't get in trouble. I wasn't even dressed. I was in my nightgown, and it was pouring rain outside. We ran downstairs. We knew about some valuables hidden in the laundry room by the other man who had been hiding there sometimes, so we thought we could grab them on the way out since we had nothing else. So the three of us ran down the stairs; thank goodness my daughter was still staying with Marisha. When we got to the door that led to the outside, it was locked so we couldn't get out. It was a big apartment building, and by this time many people were on the stairs watching us try to escape.

To make it look like we had a reason to be going downstairs, my husband said, "Come, we have to help with the suitcases." When we saw the door was locked, we went all the way down into the basement, and went into the toilet, where there was a small window. We sat there for an hour trying to figure out where to go. We had no shoes on, and I was in my nightgown. We had no money and no clothes because we ran out fast. We decided to try and escape through the bathroom window, but we heard the SS men coming down to the basement and they opened the door and found us. They took Mr. Goodman to Aschwitz. He eventually escaped but then was shot in the street and did not survive.

I don't know why the SS men didn't take us away, but they didn't. The maid brought our shoes, my pocketbook, and a few other things, and asked us not to come back. She said, "If you find a place to stay, send someone back to find out what happened to us." They arrested her in the morning. We picked up Renee, and Marisha let us stay in her basement until morning. She had a crazy sister and said if her sister heard Renee call us mom or dad, she would see that something was wrong and might report us, so we had to leave.

1944: Meeting Mrs. David

While Erwin tried to find a place for us to stay, I stayed with the Polish woman, and I told Renee not to call me Mom. She was very smart, so she knew what to do.

My husband was often sent to the Gestapo to fix cars. Every time he worked there, Mrs. David, a woman who lived in the building, came out. She was afraid to talk to the men, but eventually started talking to my husband, and he told her he had a wife and child in the lager. She was sympathetic to him. She had a big heart for the Jews. She asked how he had a wife in the lager with him? He explained that I was a dressmaker and I fixed the uniforms for the police and SS men. She said that if we were ever in danger, we could knock on her door. She always brought something for Renee.

We kept looking for a place to stay. The gardener's wife said we couldn't go there because her brother was in the army and if he came home, we could get caught. But she suggested another place. She said they could help with food but she could not hide us.

One day, the Germans announced there were two partisans in the neighborhood. German officers were in the town, and someone probably came to buy fruits and vegetables at the same time my husband was there and reported him. Right away, there were 15-20 police on bicycles surrounding the garden. My husband and his friend ran the other way to a farm, and since my husband grew up nearby, everyone knew him, so they found a place to hide. But then they got caught.

The woman we were staying with didn't know what to do. She was afraid she would be killed for hiding us. So she asked us to leave. I took my daughter to another woman's house. She gave me some bread and walked me to Mrs. David's house. I had never met her, but she knew my husband. It was very late, and very dark. The other woman came with me just in case she wasn't able to take me in.

I will never forget the sight when she opened the door. Regina David was quite the sight. She had a cigarette hanging out of her mouth, and she said, "What do you want?" My heart was pounding, and I told her my name, and that my husband was Erwin and he told me that if I was even in danger I should come here and I would be safe.

She said "Come in, come in!" so we went in. I couldn't even talk, I was crying and very upset because I thought my husband had been killed and I had nowhere to go. She told the other woman who brought me there not to worry about me, she would take care of me for as long as she could. She gave me a little room in her house, with one bed. I was so upset and crying. She told me to lie down, so I went into the bed and cried and cried. Eventually I must have fallen asleep. The next thing I remember, I opened my eyes and my husband was there.

This happened so long ago and we lived together for so many years after that, but at that moment I didn't know if I was dreaming or maybe I was in heaven or someone hit me over the head and I was imagining this, but it was real and we were together again. We talked all night, I told him I never thought I would see him again. He said that they almost got caught. They were hiding at the farm and two or three policemen arrived on bikes, so his friend went under one bed, and he went under the other bed, and the farmer said he didn't see anyone. The police asked if he had a bicycle because one of theirs broke down, so he gave him a bike and they left. The farmer said he could not keep them in the house, but they could stay in the barn in the hay. Everyone was so afraid of getting caught.

They stayed there for three days. Every morning the farmer brought them water to wash their faces, and food, and they made a hole in the hay so that if someone came in they would not see them. After three days, the farmer said, you need to figure out what to do. We didn't know how long the war would last. They decided to come back. The man gave them a little money, and the farmer's daughter walked them to the train.

Although everyone knew my husband, no one knew Mr. Lerner, my husband's friend, and he did not look Jewish. They went on the train, and had a lot of ration cards because so many people put ration cards in his pockets. Everyone knew my husband and his family because my father-in-law used to help all the farmers with their sick animals for free. He was always willing to help the farmers. My father-in-law was the only kosher butcher in the neighborhood. So my husband came to where we were, and the woman told him we were at Mrs. David's house, so they found us and stayed with us that night. In the morning, Mrs. David came into the basement, where everyone had a separate area. I wish she was alive now because Israel gives special awards and honors to people who helped the Jewish people but she died before that started.

Mrs. David was a truck driver. Her husband, a mechanic and a driver, worked for the Gestapo. They caught people who were against the Gestapo and put them in the trucks and took them to Auschwitz. Since he was the driver, he did what he could to save some of the people. He wanted to help everyone. He was a tall man and liked to do good deeds.

Many people shared the basement space. There were no walls, just partitions, made with very heavy paper. There was an area to wash clothes in another section of the basement. She told us that if someone came down to the laundry area, we must stop talking and be very quiet.

Everyone else slept in the basement but she always brought me upstairs to sleep. She had a granddaughter in the house too. Her daughter worked for a company associated with the army. Whenever she heard about people getting shot or sent to prison for helping Jews, she came home and told her mother that it was very dangerous and she should not be hiding Jews.

She put a sign in her window that people/police/soldiers were welcome to sleep in her house, and since she lived on a main street, many people came and stayed there. She had a barracks in her house for people to sleep. She wanted to show that she was a good German woman. She cooked whatever she could, and my husband helped by sending her to the farmers he knew so they would give her some food.

Eventually my daughter came and stayed with us. Mrs. David took my daughter to the farmers sometimes. They always sent us potatoes or milk or butter. The farmers always lived better than the city people because they had their own resources for food.

Eventually there were more and more people staying in the basement. One woman worked in a hat factory, one worked where they made bras, another was a dressmaker. Mrs. David tried to put everyone in the basement.

She always made coffee and baked something, she was so good to everyone. Mrs. David was always smoking like a man. My husband never smoked before, but then he started smoking.

No one knew we were in the basement because they could not see us. I did see other people who lived upstairs because I helped her with things, and she told everyone I was a Polish maid. If they ever asked about my daughter, she told them Renee was orphaned when her family was killed, and Mrs. David was looking after her. No one knew she was my daughter. Often, people wanted to adopt Renee, and Mrs. David said maybe I should give her away so she can have a better life but I did not want to be separated from my child.

We had to be very resourceful to make it work in the basement. In old Europe, potatoes came in large boxes, and Mrs. David had a big stack of these boxes in the basement, so we turned them into beds. She told us that if something bad happened upstairs and she needed to warn us, she would bang on the floor of her apartment, which was directly above the basement room. The problem was, we had no place to hide, so the men dug a hole in the corner, where the boxes were stacked. We had to sneak the dirt outside using buckets. At night, we took the dirt to the park and dumped it out. It took about two weeks to dig a hole large enough to hide in. They put the big potato boxes on top of the hole to hide it. This was only for emergencies. My husband made hinges on the box so it was like a trap door. Even if someone searched the basement, they would only see the empty box. We practiced so many times going into that hole, so we were good at it. But we never had to use it, thank goodness.

We were there for about six months. In the spring, we found out that the Russians were pushing from one side, Americans from another side, and England from another side, so they started to evacuate Auschwitz, and we were only 12 miles from Auschwitz so they marched right by us. We found out about the marches from Mrs. David because Mr. David still worked for the Gestapo. We knew people were running away because the help was getting closer. During the war, we could never understand why America didn't come to help us. We were always waiting for America to come and help. We often saw airplanes in the sky, and we prayed for America to help us.

1945: Liberation!

In January of 1945, we started to feel the excitement that something was happening. From the small basement windows, my husband and his friends saw people we knew riding by on horse and buggy.

Mrs. David told us that if German soldiers came to the house, we should go into the basement. One day, we heard the sounds of shooting, and found out that the Russians were on the other side of the river. They took over Auschwitz and were coming closer to us. We didn't know what would happen. She told us to be prepared to run just in case. Nothing happened that day, but one day at the end of January she came to the basement and said "Children, get dressed because there are 25 German soldiers in my house and they will sleep in the living room for two hours because the Russians are on their way." We could not go into the hole in the basement to hide because the soldiers might want to shoot from the windows that were located in that part of the basement, and we would get caught. So we got dressed and went to the other side of the basement by the laundry room. Just then, a bomb landed on the house and the chimney fell straight through the floor into the room where we were just seconds earlier. The soldiers had been sleeping upstairs in the room where the bomb fell, and all 25 soldiers were killed instantly. They didn't have time to escape. At 6:00 in the morning, we went upstairs and saw the dead men under the rubble. It was horrific. We watched them get carried out to the street. If we had stayed on the other side of the basement, where the hole was, we would have all been dead.

It's hard to describe what I saw or how I felt. Still today I feel like it was just a dream. All 25 soldiers were either dead or severely injured. This all happened on February 10, 1945. My mother also died on February 10, and I got my citizen papers on February 10. It is a special day for me.

Once it got quiet, Mrs. David told us it was all clear and we were allowed to go outside. The Russian soldiers were everywhere. Liberation was happening, but we had nothing to wear, and we were filthy. Mrs. David told us to take a bath, so she warmed her kettle and we took turns. And she washed our clothes. She was such a good provider for us.

I was 32 at the time, but very skinny, since we had next to nothing to eat for a few years. Somehow, I stayed strong when I was on my own and had to provide for my daughter. I embroidered her name and my aunt's name and address who lived in Brazil on a little pouch of white cotton, so just in case something happened, she would have a place to go. I always told her that if I should die, and she lived, don't go with anyone. Try to find my aunt in Brazil and she will raise you. But we pulled through because of Mrs. David.

After we washed and put on clean clothes, we wandered down to the factory near where we lived for two years, where the Germans stored flour. Many trucks were there. German flags were thrown away or burned. We moved closer to see what they were doing. We were so weak by that time because we didn't have much food. We spoke German but also understood Yiddish.

The Russians were all drunk. One of them said,"Don't go in that direction, go to the west if you can." He asked if we wanted a sack of flour or sugar but they were too heavy to lift. So one of our friends grabbed a flag from across the street. We put some flour and sugar in it and we each held a corner and carried it to Mrs. David's house. We went back to get more but the Russian man was gone, and there were no more sacks. Mrs. David was angry. She did not understand why one of us didn't wait there to guard the sacks until the others came back. But it was too late.

We stayed at Mrs. David's house for three months after the liberation, because she was afraid something might happen to us. The Russians took everything from her and she didn't speak Russian so she was afraid of them. Our friends started coming back to the area. In May, we rented a flat near Mrs. David. She had grown very close to us, and didn't want us to be too far away. I got pregnant almost right away and gave birth to my daughter Hanna about nine months after the liberation. I didn't even know I was pregnant until I was six months along. I felt sick so eventually I went to the doctor and he told me I was pregnant. I told him I was not able to carry a baby because I was too weak and could he do something about it? He said no, I have to have the baby because there aren't many Jews left and we need to repopulate, so I gave birth to Hanna. For seven months she was with Mrs. David because I didn't have any food or milk for her.

Eventually we emigrated back to Poland. Many people got shot when they came back to their homes, so my husband was afraid to go back there.

1946: Post-liberation Struggles

In 1946, we left Poland for Czechoslovakia with false Polish papers. We had Polish friends who worked in the government offices and they made false papers for us so we could go over the border. We wanted to emigrate, but it was impossible to go anywhere from Poland. We found out that Czechoslovakia had the Haganah [organization to help bring Jews to Palestine] but Poland had no resources to help people.

My brother Eric came back from Czechoslovakia a year before. He was allowed to go back to Czechoslovakia, and could go on the regular papers with his boxes of stuff. My brother got married in the lager, and he had an apartment in Czechoslovakia so I brought the little possessions I had to him.

We went to Czechoslovakia with just a little suitcase and never went back to Poland. We stayed with my brother, near the Polish border, in Slovakia. Many people went to Prague and took advantage of the Haganah program, created to help people emigrate to Israel. On August 1, 1946, we went to Austria. Our goal was to emigrate to America, but we weren't allowed to emigrate to America if we were in Poland after the war so we didn't put that on our papers. We said we were liberated elsewhere. We were with my brother for one week, and then the Jewish Community Center helped us get a train to Prague. We stayed in a refugee camp near Prague, waiting to walk through the forest over the border to Germany once they had enough people to make the trip.

One night we were told there were enough people to make the trip. It was a very difficult journey. Hanna was eight months old, and Renee was nine. With Hanna wrapped in a blanket, and Renee carrying two suitcases, we marched all night through the woods. In the morning, we came upon a house. The boy guiding us approached the house to find out where we were. He discovered we had gone in the wrong direction. Instead of walking over the border into Germany, we had gone further inside Czechoslovakia. So we had to walk all night, again, back to where we started. I don't know how we survived.

A week later, another truck came and the Haganah staff bribed the police on the border to let us through. They brought us over the border to Ash, Germany, during the night, in a big truck. They gave us some food there, and then they took us to Hoff, Germany.
[In 1945, Hoff suffered minor destruction due to aerial attacks but by the end of 1945 housed twice its previous population, receiving German-speaking refugees from neighboring Bohemia, where extensive ethnic cleansing of Czechoslovakia's German-speaking population was taking place.]

We ended up in another refugee camp in Hoff, surrounded by wire fences, with hundreds of people. They didn't know where to put everyone. My brother-in-law, Max, who also emigrated from Poland, was with us. He had been in Buchenwald, then came to stay with us. *[**Buchenwald** (German pronunciation: [ˈbuːxn̩valt]; literally 'beech forest') was a Nazi concentration camp established on Ettersberg Hill near Weimar, Germany, in July 1937. It was one of the first and the largest of the concentration camps within the Altreich.]* He looked terrible; such a contrast from before the war, when he was a very good-looking man.

Hoff was worse than anywhere else. Hanna was just a baby, and we had no diapers, only rags to put on her, and no money, although there was no place to buy anything anyway. There was no hot water, and it was very

63

cold there. To get food, we had to stand in line at a window every day, just like during the war. Everyone had a bucket, and they gave us the food through the window. It was terrible.

Often, I had to send Renee to get the food, but she was just nine years old, and small. My husband was gone most of the time, because he was trying to find an apartment for us. The conditions were terrible; we slept in a barracks with many other people. There was no communication. Everyone was hungry and out for themselves. We were there for about two months, and Renee rarely got food from the window because she was small and other people would reach over and take the food from her.

Somehow we survived. We never found an apartment, because we had no money. Although my husband had the courage to push us through the rough times, he wasn't so good with getting money. Finally, he saw a notice that there was space for 20 families to resettle somewhere, so we signed up because we needed to get out of there. Our group was made up of mostly Polish people.

We ended up in Landau, on the Isar river, between Munich and Reigensborg in late 1946. We got a room. We stayed there from 1946 - 1948. In 1948, the Gichner family, Erwin's distant cousins, sent us papers to emigrate to the United States. We filled out the paperwork, and got checked by the doctor, but then found out that the quotas were filled, so we could not go after all. We were very disappointed.

We had the option of going to Brazil to live with my aunt, as long as my husband could prove he was a craftsman. He went through the certification and was approved. But then my aunt told us that in order for us to go there, we had to go to a priest and get papers saying we had "converted" to Catholicism, because they did not want to let Jews in. She said that once we arrived, we could go back to being Jewish.

My husband refused. "No. I will not do that. We survived the war, as Jews, and we will find a way to start a new life. But I will not say I am Catholic." In the end, it was good that we didn't go because my aunt died, and my uncle left Brazil and went to Israel.

My niece, Herta, decided to go to Israel with the Haganah, and we decided to apply to go to Israel too, and give up on our dream of coming to America. We worked on our application, and got ready to pack, but then they opened up the quotas again for America so we decided to try one more time, and we got approved. We made the voyage across the ocean to America in April, 1949, but it was a very difficult journey.

1949: The Journey to America

We stayed in another DP (displaced persons) camp in Berhman for two weeks. Again, we waited in line for food. The men were separated from the women. It was awful. Every day we went to the office to see if our names were on the list. Finally, after two weeks, we saw our names on the list for a boat called Haan, named after General Haan. *[USS General W. G. Haan (AP-158) was a General G. O. Squier-class transport ship for the U.S. Navy in World War II. She was named in honor of U.S. Army general William George Haan. On December 18, 1949, she left Bremerhaven, Germany, arriving December 28 in New York City with mostly Polish passengers. Military Wiki.]*

We were so relieved to finally get out of Germany, but the journey was terrible. It was December and the weather was very bad. Many boats started out and then had to turn back because the water was so rough. Our boat, which came from Brazil, was very old and meant for only 400 people, but there were 1150 people on the voyage. Everyone was together; the kitchen staff, the boat crew, Ukrainians, and Polish people. I was lucky because I had two children, so I was assigned a cabin, which I shared with another woman who had a child. The cabin was tiny, with two double beds. We shared a toilet with other people on the boat. The men were not allowed to come into the cabins. Every morning we were told to leave our cabin and get on the deck, but we didn't want to go outside because we were all so sick from the rough seas, and it was cold and nasty and rainy outside. All the kids were crying, and we had little food. The journey lasted for 11 miserable days. My husband helped clean the toilets. Everyone who was able helped with something.

The boat took us to Boston, where we had to go through another medical exam. They took us aside and said we did not pass the evaluation because our lungs were not clear, and said we had to go back to Germany. After waiting five years to emigrate, with two little kids, and a terrible journey on the ship, we were devastated.

We did not want to go back to Germany. It was totally chaotic there. People were fighting and screaming at each other, and there were black markets everywhere. Everyone was against each other. We didn't want to get involved in black market activity because we were afraid we would get into trouble. It was so stressful. I prayed for my children to live, they didn't do anything wrong.

So when we failed the medical exam, we lost all hope. They kept us for three or four hours on the side, trying to decide what to do with us. It was 4:00 in the morning, and we didn't know what to do. We had nowhere to go if we went back because our apartment was probably already taken by another family.

Before we left Germany, my cousin, Margot Friedlander, who lived in NY, wrote that she would pick us up when we got off the boat, but she wasn't there. That just added to our stress and confusion about what to do.

I was crying constantly, and my husband had a very bad headache. Finally, after four hours, another officer came by and looked at the evaluation again. He said, "She's 50% and he's 50%, so just let them in."

I think he felt sorry for us. We were so relieved.

While we were trying to figure out what to do next, the kids were curious about their surroundings. Renee asked for Coca-cola, even though she didn't know what it was, and Hanna wanted to try a banana because she saw someone eating one on the boat. Everyone got $2, from Hias [*HIAS* is the **Hebrew Immigrant Aid Society**[4], *a Jewish American nonprofit organization that provides humanitarian aid and assistance to refugees.]* so we had a total of $8. I found a banana and a cola for the kids, but the banana was green, so Hanna wouldn't eat it because it tasted terrible, and I didn't know that green bananas taste bad. Renee didn't like coca-cola either. She thought it would taste better.

We didn't know where we were going, and Erwin's headache was so bad, he couldn't do much of anything except lie down. My cousin never came, and since I didn't speak English, it was hard to find someone to help us. Eventually, we found out there was a letter waiting for us from my cousin. She said she was in New York, and was working, and it was too far to come to Boston, but she would see us when we got to Washington. So now we had to figure out how to get to Washington, but first I needed to get help for my husband, who was feeling so sick he could hardly see. I heard someone speaking Polish, so I asked if she could help my husband because of his terrible headache. She gave him something, maybe an aspirin, and he felt a little bit better. At 6:00 PM we boarded the train to Washington.

We arrived in Washington at 5:00 AM. When we got off the train, a lady was calling our name, and she spoke a little bit of Yiddish. Mrs. Gichner (a distant cousin) had asked her friend to get us into a taxi and send us to her house on Highland Place in Washington, near 34th street. The taxi driver had no idea where it was. He asked people on the street, but it was 5:00 AM and not many people were around. Eventually he found it. He knocked on the door, and Mrs. Gichner came out. We were a bit shocked at her appearance; she was very old, and hunched over.

We got out of the car with the little baggage we had and went into her house. She made us Matzo Brei *[small pieces of matzo soaked in water, mixed with beaten eggs, and fried.]* because it was Passover and she was religious. The kids had their own room, and we had our own room, for the first time ever. We were so relieved to have a place to stay. The house was very nice, and filled with expensive things like artwork and vases. Unfortunately, it was not very suitable for little children. Hanna was around three years old. She was a tomboy, and could not sit still for five minutes, so I had to keep a close eye on her so she didn't break anything. It was very stressful, because their house was like a museum.

We were grateful to have food after going so long without much to eat, but the food was strange to the kids, so they didn't want to eat anything. Mrs. Gichner was very bossy, and said I should force them to eat. Everything was so elegant, and she even had a maid.

Because Hanna was so small, she had to kneel in the chair to reach the table, and she knocked over a glass a couple of times by accident. One time, when this happened, I took her upstairs and spanked her but I felt terrible about it. I told my husband we needed to get out of there. Everything was polished, and the floors were slippery. It was not a place for little kids. A few times, Hanna slid down the banister on her stomach! There were two big vases on the steps, and when Mrs. Gichner saw her doing that, she yelled, "She needs to stop or else she will get hurt!" But I'm pretty sure she was more worried about her vases than she was about Hanna.

About two weeks later, we found an apartment near Connecticut Ave. and S Street. We lived there for four years, but my husband had a very hard time finding a job, because when people asked who sponsored him to come to America and he told them the Gichners, they all said Mr. Gichner should help him, since he is very wealthy.

Erwin's brother, Max, arrived in America around the same time we did. He was very smart, and spoke eight languages. He said he was a craftsman so they gave him a job in the factory, but after a few days, they saw that he didn't know what he was doing, so they told him he had to find another job.

Max, Herta's father, came from Germany, wanted to go to Israel, but he wasn't very healthy, and since Israel needed able-bodied people to help build things up, that wasn't a good option for him, so he came to America instead.

My husband was very handy, and eventually found odd jobs. He worked for a painter, he scraped floors, and slowly worked himself up and eventually worked for Lawrence Gichner as a roofer. He had a hard time because everyone knew he was connected to the Gichners so they gave him the worst jobs.

It was not what he expected, so eventually he started working for himself as a roofer, but roofing is a tough business and Erwin had trouble with his arm because of injuries during the war. We were looking for other ways to make an income, so when some friends told us they were starting a chicken farm in Philadelphia, we decided to raise chickens too. We borrowed money from the Gichners and bought a chicken farm in New Jersey, and moved there. We stayed for five years, but it wasn't working out, so we came back to Washington and he went back to roofing, and started making artwork out of metal.

He was really an artist at heart. He made menorahs for the Smithsonian and for the White House, and was invited to the State House in Annapolis. He made and donated menorahs to local synagogues and Yeshivas *[a traditional Jewish educational institution focused on the study of Rabbinic literature]* He had a workshop in Kensington, MD, and was happy creating wall sconces, metal sculptures, and many menorahs. Years later, he had his first heart attack, but recovered. Then he had another heart attack, and they did an operation to fix his heart, but they gave him bad blood and he got hepatitis and died. It was tragic. After all we went through; surviving the war, the beatings, near starvation, being in prison and the work camps…and then this happened.

He started making the menorahs during the war. He was a foreman for two and a half years in the first lager, in Belitz, so we were there through Hanukkah. He found scraps of wire and nails and made a menorah out of them, so we could light the menorah at Hanukkah if we could find old candles.When he set up a workshop in Maryland, he made Menorahs in his spare time between roofing jobs. Eventually, he had enough customers and did it full time. The designs were based on the designs he made during the war.

People ask if I have bad feelings about the Germans. We had many difficult experiences and encountered many bad people during the war; but we also found people who helped us, and that partially made up for the bad people. The good people saved our lives by giving us food and a place to hide, and even the bad SS man tried to help us in some ways. Maybe we were spared because my husband was a good worker and did everything they asked. I also worked hard; I never said no, except the one time I mentioned earlier, when they told me to get dressed because they were taking us to Auschwitz and I said, "No, I will not get dressed. Shoot me here if you need to. I am not going."

Sadly, my father-in-law was killed just two weeks before the liberation. He was very sick and was hiding at a farm so he could rest and get better, but someone saw him and reported him. The Germans found him and tied up his legs and put him on the train to Auschwitz. Later, we found out he died on the train and never made it to Auschwitz. But it probably didn't matter, he would have been killed once he got there.

Follow-up: Life in America

After the war, some friends told my husband that they would give him the names of the people who turned in my father-in-law and killed him. They said, "You can kill them and we will not punish you." My husband said, "No, I will not do that. If God wants to punish them, let him. You cannot do bad for bad. If someone throws a stone at you, take a piece of bread and throw it back. Show them a better way." My husband was so good natured, like my mother and father, who did good things in the community to help our neighbors. Maybe that's why we survived.

Everyone talked so nicely about Erwin at his funeral. I received so many letters from old friends, thanking him for all the nice things he did, and for the beautiful artwork he made.

My oldest daughter, Renee, married a Jewsh man, Boris, and although they belonged to a temple and their children went to Hebrew School, she didn't practice the religion like she did before they were married. When we came to the United States she was more religious. My husband was very religious and he taught the children as well.

Along with everyone else, our grandchildren loved spending time with my husband because he was such a kind soul, and he taught them how to be good to people. He said "Don't hate anyone, and always do the right thing" I try to follow this as well. I don't live for myself, I live for my family, but I worry that I am the last one to keep the family so close together.

Every day I get letters from friends all over the world, who also survived the war. I don't write letters so much anymore, because every time I get a letter from certain people, I get very emotional and I cry for hours. My friends ask if I remember things from the war. I do, but I try to push those memories out of my mind, because it's too painful to remember.

War reparations *[War reparations are compensation payments made after a war by one side to the other, intended to cover damage or injury inflicted during a war]*

I eventually received restitution from the Germans. I didn't get anything for the months I was in hiding, but I got money for the time I was in the ghetto and the lagers and working for the SS man. They said if you are not well, you can apply for additional compensation, so I applied, due to increasing anxiety from being in the war. My husband was compensated for that as well. At first, I did not want to see the doctors because I had such bad experiences during the war with doctors and I did not trust them. But a friend convinced me to go. The doctor asked me so many questions, it made me crazy. I didn't even know what I was talking about, I got all mixed up with my answers to certain things. In the end, he put down that I had trouble with my nerves, so I got 25% additional restitution.

Talking about the war

I didn't talk to my children about the war for a long time because Renee did not want to talk about it, and whenever she saw my crying about the war she said "Mom, stop, you don't have to say anything, you don't have to talk about it, and many people don't believe us anyway, because the things that happened to us are beyond belief." No one believed that I saved a child in the lager, because all the children were killed. I was one in thousands that saved a child in the lager. If a child survived, usually it was because they were hiding in the forest or somewhere else, but not in the lager. It was never heard of. Even when I was working for the SS man, she was with me. People said he was one of the worst but he wasn't so bad to me. I was sewing day and night, and doing whatever they asked. Make a uniform, a coat, whatever. I don't know how I did it. You did not talk about this with your children. My grandchildren were so happy to hear that I was being interviewed because they wanted to know what happened. Renee never spoke to her kids about the war, and she died when she was 44 years old from cancer, so they never learned what happened. She could not bring herself to tell her children about it, but now that I am older and I see my friends dying, I believe it's important for my family to know something about what happened.

Does the war still affect you?
I still have dreams about it, and sometimes I wake up in the middle of the night and I am not sure where I am. What bothers me the most is when Renee saw the SS men take those pregnant girls away. I could never get over that, and I'm not sure she ever did either. I didn't even want to look at him. But I had no choice, I had to see him every day because I was working for him and if I refused to do the work, he would probably kill me too. I know it affected Renee, she was always crying because the Jewish woman who worked in the kitchen scared her when she didn't want to babysit. She said "Your mother is gone and the devil took her already and she is dead." So sometimes, when I came home late and she was sleeping on the floor, I woke her up and she said, "Mommy, you are here!" she couldn't believe it because that woman told her I was dead. I am grateful my other children didn't have to deal with that.

So Renee always said, "Mom, don't talk about it, forget about it. We are in America, we have a different life now." She went to school in Washington. Renee was very smart. She attended English classes for six weeks, and then went to regular school. She was a great student even though she never attended school before. She never went to college, but she worked for the Telephone Company for 25 years

Anything else you want to share?
When I was 42, I had my third child, Julie. Times were tough because the chicken farm wasn't doing well, and we owed money to the

Gichners. So when I got pregnant, I was surprised, and it was a hard time. Renee was just getting married. My three daughters were ten years apart. I also helped raise my grandchildren, but now my nerves are shot and it's too hard. Renee was closest to my heart because we went through so much together. I try to help the children and grandchildren as much as I can. They have good husbands and my grandchildren admire me. I miss my husband very much. I don't know if I should sell the house, but I don't want to move because then I have to throw everything out and I don't want to do that, he worked so hard for everything. I am not a youngster anymore, but I like to travel.

When we first moved to America, I was still sewing, but now I manage with social security and a little money from Germany. I do what I can afford and if I can't afford it, I skip it. I never buy things I cannot afford. I only hope my children will be good to me, and will never forget me and be good people. I hope my grandchildren do good in their lives. We always tried to be polite and not hate anyone.

I hope I don't suffer like my daughter did when she died, she was very sick for two years. And I hope my children never have to experience what we went through. I don't care for luxury, I just want to have peace, and die peacefully, and I think everyone wants that, because we can't be here forever. Everyone has to go someday. You can't choose when you will leave this earth. I hope I didn't hurt anyone in my life. I am thankful for every day. My husband went to synagogue and prayed every day. I am only sorry I didn't record what the Rabbi said about him at his funeral; he praised him so highly. My husband was a very good man. And I hope my children will never forget about their parents. I wish I could be with him now, but I will be there someday. Thank you for listening.

Notes from the author

Growing up, I was aware of the Holocaust, but didn't know the details about how my mom and grandparents survived until my grandmother was interviewed by the Shoah Foundation.

As I listened to her tell these stories, I was shaken to the core at how many times she, my mother, and my grandfather came close to death, and then somehow survived to see another day. I had no idea how rare it was for a child to survive the Holocaust. This knowledge gave me pause and made me realize that my existence is a direct result of my grandparents' grit, determination and resourcefulness. That, along with the assistance of a few very brave citizens who risked their lives to help, they survived.

Once they emigrated to the United States, it took them a few years to find their way, but after some struggles, they settled in Silver Spring, Maryland. Erwin continued making menorahs and other metal sculptures, went to the synagogue every day, and led a simple, peaceful life. Hilda worked part time, stayed active in the Jewish community and loved spending time with her grandchildren and later, her great-grandchildren. I had the opportunity to travel to Israel with Hilda in 1988, a life-long dream for her and for me.

Sadly, Renee, their daughter, my mom, passed away at the age of 44 from cancer. This was devastating to the entire family, but especially to Hilda because they went through so much during the war. Hilda lived to the age of 94 and maintained her generosity, positive attitude, and focus on her family until the very end. We all miss her very much.

Appendix

What is a lager?

Arbeitslager is a German language word which means labor camp. Under Nazism, the German government (and its private-sector, Axis, and collaborator partners) used forced labor extensively, starting in the 1930s but most especially during World War II. Another term was *Zwangsarbeitslager* "forced labor camp."

The Nazis operated several categories of *Arbeitslager* for different categories of inmates. The largest number of them held civilians forcibly abducted in the occupied countries (see Łapanka for Polish context) to provide labor in the German war industry, repair bombed railroads and bridges, or work on farms and in stone quarries.[1]

Lager is the name the Jewish prisoners most often use to describe the concentration camps, like Auschwitz. More than simply describing the physical location, the term Lager also embodies the dehumanization and cruelty wrought upon the Jewish prisoners by the Germans in the camp.

Source: WIkipedia

Photographs

Bielitz Lager, concentration camp, 1942.
Renee is front and center, surrounded by the other men in the camp, and Erwin.
She was 5 years old.

Hilda, Erwin, & Renee
Bielitz Lager
1942

Hilda and Erwin

Renee in Landau, Germany,
1947

Hilda

Erwin, Hilda, Hanna, Renee

Renee, Hanna, Hilda

Erwin's sibling. Erwin is likely the
second from the Right

Hermina (Erwin's sister)
Hilda, Julie.
Chicken Farm in Freehold,
NJ

Circa 1918: Julius, Hilda, Eric and
Rosa Goldberger

Erwin

Erwin

Annie Goldberger
(Hilda's sister)

Hanna, Julie, Renee
Julie's Wedding,
1979 Maryland

Erwin and Hilda
1975
40 year wedding anniversary
Damascus, MD

•

Made in the USA
Middletown, DE
30 December 2024

68528019R00046